LEADERSHIP
FROM THE HEART OF A COACH!

L. Dennis "Coach D" Robinson

Published by LDR & Associates
LEADERSHIP ACADEMY

and

TRAFFORD

• Canada • UK • Ireland • USA

[Handwritten inscription: Ernie, God Bless you! Richest. I pray All of God's Richest Blessings be upon you! You are A great Ambassador of Christ! We will be Friends for life. Always remember to give God All the Glory! Remember MPH 5:16 Coach]

Scripture taken from the HOLY BIBLE, NEW INTERNATIONAL VERSION®. Copyright © 1973, 1978, 1984 International Bible Society. Used by permission of Zondervan. All rights reserved.
The "NIV" and "New International Version" trademarks are registered in the United States Patent and Trademark Office by International Bible Society. Use of either trademark requires the permission of International Bible Society.

Note for Librarians: A cataloguing record for this book is available from Library and Archives Canada at www.collectionscanada.ca/amicus/index-e.html
ISBN 1-4120-8913-1

Printed in Victoria, BC, Canada. Printed on paper with minimum 30% recycled fibre.
Trafford's print shop runs on "green energy" from solar, wind and other environmentally-friendly power sources.

Published by LDT & Associates,Leadership Academy P.O. Box 910513, Lexington, KY 40591
Photography by Harkert Studio, Milan, IL

Offices in Canada, USA, Ireland and UK

Book sales for North America and international:
Trafford Publishing, 6E–2333 Government St.,
Victoria, BC V8T 4P4 CANADA
phone 250 383 6864 (toll-free 1 888 232 4444)
fax 250 383 6804; email to orders@trafford.com
Book sales in Europe:
Trafford Publishing (UK) Limited, 9 Park End Street, 2nd Floor
Oxford, UK OX1 1HH UNITED KINGDOM
phone +44 (0)1865 722 113 (local rate 0845 230 9601)
facsimile +44 (0)1865 722 868; info.uk@trafford.com
Order online at:
trafford.com/06-0669

10 9 8 7 6 5 4 3 2

TABLE OF CONTENTS

DEDICATION

This may appear to be an unusual dedication, but I want to thank some people who have given their time and efforts to make my dream a reality.

First and foremost, I want to thank my Lord God of the heavens above for sending down His Son, my Savior Jesus Christ, to die on the cross so that my sins would be forgiven. Because of His love, I will be sharing eternal life in heaven with His Son Jesus, who rose from the dead on the third day!

I would also like to dedicate this book in loving memory to my beloved mother, Evelyn Ruth Robinson, my darling grandmother Mary Ann Robinson and my adoring sister, Shirley Robinson ... they are all so precious to me.

Then I wish to thank my family and friends for all of their encouraging words and opinions. I could name each of you, and say some great things, but you all know who you are. I will say, though, that my sister-in-law Tracy's sharp wit saved me a lot of embarrassing moments before publication. Thank you, Sis!

And of course my darling wife, Tammy; the whole

book belongs to her. Her patience and efforts gave me an overwhelming amount of energy to its completion ... she is a jewel. She never once complained or became upset about all of the time I spent writing and rewriting this book. As newlyweds, of course, time is of the essence – and Tammy was generous with our time. Another way that my lovely wife added to this book was as a one-woman advertisement. She would talk, and brag on me and about me, and promote this book to anyone who will listen. I love you so much, Darling!

Last but not least, I'd like to thank my great friend and editor, Rev. Brian Kinney, whose patience, understanding, and overwhelming love for our Lord allowed me to express myself in a professional manner utilizing his already proven success, professionalism, and talents. Brian, my friend, you are a Godsend!

I thank God and the Holy Spirit for guiding me to you. It brings to life Jeremiah 29:11: "For I know the plans I have for you," declares the LORD, "plans to prosper you and not to harm you, plans to give you hope and a future." Brian, you will forever be my brother in Christ. May God's richest blessings be upon you, and everyone associated with my life and this book. This includes everyone who reads it, be it past, present, or future. Until we rejoice in eternity, to God be ALL of the glory!

Amen! Coach "D"

Leadership is a quality that is difficult to define, let alone acquire. Any definition is usually influenced heavily by the biases of the person doing the defining. We might say that defining leadership is a bit like defining art. As the saying goes, "I don't know what art is, but I know it when I see it." That sort of statement may end the discussion about defining art or leadership, but it is not helpful in the least for those of us who need leaders, or want to be leaders, in a world that seems desperately short of people we want to follow.

Recently The New York Times announced the resignation of Dr. Lawrence H. Summers as president of Harvard University after a five-year tenure. The Times wrote: "Hailed in his first days as a once-in-a-century leader ... Dr. Summers, 51, came into office with plans to expand the campus, put new focus on undergraduate education and integrate the university's schools. But he eventually alienated professors with a personal style that many saw as bullying and arrogant ... some of his major decisions ... were

hugely divisive at the 370-year-old university." One
of the professors at Harvard remarked to the Times,
"A strong leader is not just someone who can name
a goal or force a change, but someone who can bring
out the best in people and find ways to encourage
teamwork."

Now I cannot tell you whether or not Dr. Summers' critics described him accurately. Even the best
of leaders have their critics. But most of us would
want far better results from our leaders or from our
own leadership.

In this book, Coach "D" takes a fresh look at leadership. He blows the whistle on some misconceptions
about leadership, and gets to the heart of the matter
– which IS the heart! As a devout Christian, Coach
"D" realizes that leadership is a character trait that
is basic to who we are, and it is the outpouring of a
heart committed to God. Leadership can be broken
down into its various aspects, which Coach has done
for the reader, but at its essence it is a quality of Jesus Christ, a quality which we are able to imitate
as our hearts are turned more and more toward the
heart of God.

Jesus both taught and demonstrated the idea of
servant leadership, that a leader must be willing
to serve those he leads. This requires great humility, something we don't always associate with leadership. And it requires integrity, that character trait
that transcends all others. In this book, Coach "D"
has taken the leadership qualities taught and mod-

eled by Jesus and applied them to the world of today, especially the world of our young people, and has produced an excellent guide for those who would be leaders and not simply "wannabees."

It has been my privilege to edit this book, and it is my prayer that you will glean insights here that have come from Coach's 27 years of developing leaders and being a leader.

Reverend Brian W. Kinney
Nashville, Tennessee
February 22, 2006

LEADERSHIP
... FROM THE HEART OF A COACH!

CHAPTER 1

IN THE BEGINNING

As a basketball coach and former coach in football, baseball, and track, I have come across a great many followers, but only a small number of leaders. Of all the young men and women I have coached over a 27-year career, the ratio of followers to leaders is about 80 percent to 20 percent – the 80 percent being the followers.

On the basketball court, it's easy to see the more talented athletes step up as leaders, because those roles come naturally to them. An athlete who performs well automatically has teammates who want to imitate what the star player does during the game. When a team has players who lead with their performance, it can be just as much fun to follow as it is to lead. Because of this, many athletes – and people in other walks of life as well – tend to let those naturally gifted leaders do the leading. This may be good for the team at the time but, in the long run, the followers can allow their own latent leadership abilities to go stagnant. This tendency can follow a person throughout life, and keep him or her from developing into a leader. A person who might have become a great leader is content instead with simply following someone with natural skills.

This does not have to be so. What I want to share with you in this book is that although you may have been a follower on the basketball court or some athletic field, on a playground or in a classroom, or even in the workplace, you still can become a leader in life.

Coaches have a perspective on leadership that positions them well for helping others to develop as leaders. Two coaches in particular stand out from my youth as being great in this regard. Understand that I have known many great coaches in my lifetime, and loved them all, but two were special. These two coaches influenced my life, even though they never coached me directly.

The first was Coach Doughty, my older brother's basketball coach. Every time I saw Coach Doughty, or whenever he saw me, no matter how late it was, or how much time he had or didn't have – he always took time to share a "moment" with me. Some of those "moments" took significant time from his busy schedule.

The moments we shared were special indeed. I talked ... he listened. He talked ... I listened. He modeled the very things I wanted to be when I grew up. He was smart, articulate, and well-dressed. He was understanding of my point of view, but would be sure to get his point across.

The second was Coach Cavanaugh, my older brother's high school coach and driver education instructor. What a man! His day was never too busy to help someone in need. If Coach Cavanaugh had $10.00 in his pocket and you needed it, it was yours.

That might not seem a lot to you, but when you think about it, most people get pretty stingy when they're down to their last few dollars. How many would give half their money, let alone all of it? Coach Cavanaugh never seemed even to think about asking for the money back. He was a man who just wanted to serve others.

The importance of these two coaches in my life is that they exemplified true servanthood. They always were willing to place others' needs ahead of their own. Beyond this character trait, they both had control over their tongues. I never heard any harsh words from either man toward anyone else for something that person did or didn't do. You could approach these guys about anything at all, and never hear anything harsh or resentful ... I promise you. A leader doesn't need to tear down other people, only to build up others. In the words of the Apostle Paul, "Do not let any unwholesome talk come out of your mouths, but only what is helpful for building others up according to their needs, that it may benefit those who listen." (Ephesians 4:29)

These coaches would oftentimes give up personal assets and time to assure that others less fortunate (my brothers included) could have what they needed. Coach Cavanaugh was always sensitive to how much it meant to our family of 12 kids to have someone with a license to drive, and to have a car. Just to travel back and forth from church to school to the grocery store, we needed help. Coach Cavanaugh would come to our house on the weekends with his own personal car and give my brothers driving lessons. When they were ready to test for their licenses, he would allow them to use his own car.

To top that off, there were times that Coach Doughty would drop off at our house a new pair of shoes in one of the younger kids' sizes, just to help out. Never once did he ask anything in return. He would do this with pants, shirts, and jackets, as well. He did this often, without being asked. He just knew that we would need these things. In today's world of changing regulations, coaches and others involved with sports have to be more cautious about helping families in our situation because some would see it as illegal recruiting and cite the school for recruiting violations. Trust me; this thought was far from either coach's mind. They were practicing servanthood, something that is almost a lost art! These coaches were showing a heart of true compassion. Coach Doughty would always say, "Don't worry about paying me now, pay me next time." And yes, you guessed it ... he said the same thing each time we tried to pay. I knew I wanted to be like that – to help people by serving them!

Now, I could go on about how these coaches became heroes in my eyes, but I just wanted to let you know how I learned at an early age that servanthood is the foundation of all leadership qualities. From the examples of Coach Cavanaugh and Coach Doughty, I knew that one day I would be a coach ... and help others learn how to lead and to serve. Although I was only in elementary school then, I knew that I was on to something and something big.

The world of sports can be a good arena to prepare people for leadership. But let the record show a warning, because some leaders in the sports world today truly believe – erroneously – that they are leaders in the game of life as well. I would beg to differ with them.

Many of these successful sports leaders will fail in the rest of life because they don't choose to build on their sports leadership qualities once they leave the court or the field. Regardless of their former status as leaders, they all too often fall into the category of "wannabees" in life outside the arena. A wannabee is someone who believes he or she is a leader, but isn't motivated to do the work necessary to earn that standing. Others may have thrust them into leadership roles so they could avoid that responsibility themselves. This happens often in the world of athletics.

Sometimes youth are pushed into leadership positions in the hope that somehow they will be mentored and cultivated as leaders. These youth end up with the idea that they don't have to do anything to maintain their leadership status.

Now I am sure many of you are thinking to yourselves, "I know lots of athletes who are great leaders," and that's wonderful. There certainly are some terrific examples of athletes who continued to develop as leaders beyond their years in athletics. Former athletes serve in state legislatures, Congress, and all sorts of government positions – some have been presidents of the United States – and ex-athletes turn up as leaders in businesses and industries of all sorts. They also show up as leaders in churches and other kinds of ministries, including organizations such as Athletes in Action and the Fellowship of Christian Athletes. However, it wouldn't be hard to come up with a list of names of athletes who really blew it at trying to be leaders off the court after successfully being leaders on the court or playing field. Some have ended up in crime, serving long stretches in prison. Others have been involved in drugs. Many have had failures in marriage and family as well as career. Some are just plain unpleasant people to be around.

Society has taught us to believe that if you are given the title of "leader," you must have earned it. The logic of our minds causes us to think, "If I was chosen as leader before, I must be pretty good, so I can do it on my own. I'm OK." You might then stop working at being a leader.

But unless young people are fully mentored and cultivated to become leaders and to remain leaders, they will fail in those positions, and often in life. This will keep them locked up in the continual state of mind called "wannabee." Think about it!

What do you think?

What kinds of people have you seen as leaders in your life? What is it that makes you look to them for leadership? Your thoughts:

CHAPTER 2

WANNABEES

Do you find yourself chasing after the most popular boy or girl at your school in order to improve your own image? If so, you're going to be a wannabee. Is it hard to say "no" to someone you know is doing all the wrong things for all the wrong reasons? If so, you're going to be a wannabee. Do you think "wannabee" is a term that applies to others and not to you? Do you think it's all about the other guy, and that you can't be "played" like that? Do you think it's just a word you can use to win at Scrabble? Think again!

How do I know? What makes me think I'm Mr. Know-It-All? Hello ... because I've been there. ... I've done those things. ... I was a "wannabee."

Johnny Batson was big and strong. He was a great athlete. All the girls liked him. Now me ... well ... I wore glasses. I was small. I mean, come on now, I was Theodore Cleaver from "Leave It To Beaver," Ernie Thompson Douglas from "My Three Sons," and Steve Urkel from "Family Matters," all rolled into one. I can almost hear you laughing, but that's the way it was.

So that I would fit in and be accepted, I thought I had to get into Johnny Batson's "clique." If I could just join his world, I thought, I would be somebody – I would have status. Are you with me now? Are you sensing where I'm coming from?

You might say, "But Coach D, I'm not like that! I

13

look like Denzel Washington or Brad Pitt or maybe Halle Berry, or Jennifer Aniston!" The point is, don't be fooled into thinking it's all about looks. Read on.

Thurman Bishop and Purnell Akers were star basketball players. These guys did anything and everything wrong that you could imagine in school when they were growing up. They sure could play basketball, though, and they were the captains of the varsity basketball team – they were "All-Americans." Need I say more? Everyone liked them. If you hung out with them, everyone thought you must be cool; you must be somebody worth getting to know. You know what, it didn't matter what those guys did, or what they asked me to do, hanging out with them made me cool (wannabee), and that was all that mattered at the time ... so I thought.

The truth was that I was a wannabee, just a nobody desperately looking for somebody, anybody.

Phony leaders come a dime a dozen. Everywhere you go, you see people "perpetrating," doing things wrong for attention. Why? They don't have what it takes for true leadership – or maybe no one is taking the time and making the effort to mentor them, to cultivate them.

How do you change? What can you do? What's the secret? What does it take to be a leader? Youth and parents all around the world have pondered these questions. You grow up constantly hearing comments like these from your parents and respected adults: "Johnny, you need to be more like a leader." "I want you to grow up being a leader." Or, "Susan, why can't you be more like Sharon? She's a leader." Why? Why? Why?

If your parents are like mine, they know the Scriptures, especially Proverbs 22:6.

That verse reads: "Train a child in the way he should go, and when he is old he will not turn from it." Parents understand this idea, of course, but the majority of them fail to do anything substantial to prepare their children for leadership. Why is this? It's because most parents do what their own parents did; grandparents did what their parents did, and so forth. This is how society works, and so we don't improve our leadership training from generation to generation. Youth grow up following in their parents' footsteps, and emulating them, for better or for worse.

What do you think?

What is the problem with being a "wannabee" leader? What would keep people from following such a leader? Your thoughts:

CHAPTER 3

WHAT IS LEADERSHIP?

B eing a leader is not something that comes from waving a magic wand and saying, "Abracadabra." Leaders are not overnight sensations. Leadership skills are acquired over time by utilizing certain strategies and developing specific lifestyles.

As surprising as it may seem, we all are born with certain qualities of leadership. What happens, though, is that the majority of us do not choose to build on those qualities, and we simply live out a life of following. As "wannabees," we grow up without being able to grasp our potential.

Noah Webster, author of the original 1820 American Dictionary of the English Language, defines leadership as "the position or office of a leader with the ability and capacity to lead." He describes a leader as "one that leads or guides." With that in mind, are you a leader? Before you start examining yourself, let me explain something.

Many of you who are youths get confused on this question because you have several "wannabee" peers following you around and telling you all the time that you are "all that" and a "Reese's Peanut Butter Cup." This kind of adoration makes you think that you are a leader, with leadership qualities. Hello! Do you hear me?

Just because you go to the mall and have ten little

"honeys" following you from store to store, and eight little guy "wannabees" chasing those ten little honeys, that does not make you a leader – it does not mean you have leadership qualities.

What about having six or seven other youths pile inside your car to "hang" with you? If the truth be known, the real reason they have anything to do with you in the first place is that you are blessed just to HAVE a car! The fact is that you are a chaser, a stone-cold, straight-out-of-the-book "wannabee."

Surprised? Probably so. But if you look at the mirror you will most likely see somebody who is reaching out to anyone in order to be accepted. Somewhere along the line, you have been rejected or neglected. I'm not referring just to rejection by parents. There are other ways that young people are rejected or neglected. Perhaps you were the last one chosen in a game of tag at school; perhaps you weren't chosen at all. Or, maybe everyone in your class is going to the movies, but no one asked you to go. What about the time you wanted to join a club and people made fun of you? How about when you didn't make the Little League team, or the high school football team?

Rejection and neglect can happen several ways. Some incidents are so small that they go almost unnoticed; others are quite noticeable. No matter the size of the event or whether or not slights were made knowingly or unknowingly, the rejection hurts just the same. (Of course the ones done knowingly and intentionally do hurt more; they do "cut the deepest.")

In some sense, we all experience rejection and neglect at various times in the course of life. Don't start to feel all alone because it has happened to you.

What do you do when you are rejected or neglected? You begin to reach out. You begin to latch on to anyone, anything. You begin grasping, just to be someone, just to count for something. But sometimes that person at the end of your grasp is exactly the wrong one for you, someone who will take advantage of you, maybe abuse you.

You begin to search, and usually you will find someone, somewhere in your life – or in someone else's life – that you trust. It may be someone you have known or maybe observed; someone who fits the description of what you think (the key word is "think") is a leader.

Then you begin to emulate that person, whether for good or for bad, right or wrong.

Part of the problem in all this comes from the society in which we live. Society has encouraged adults to believe that having a lot of money, or driving an expensive car, automatically makes a person a leader. Don't get me wrong; it's great to have a lot of money, and it's great to drive nice cars and have expensive things. I'd even go so far as to say that setting your lifestyle so that you'll earn these things can help to build leadership qualities. However, having these things does not, in itself, make you a leader.

Following the pattern of adults, a young person quite naturally grows up to think, "If I have a lot of money, or if I can get an expensive car, I'll be somebody. I'll be a leader. People will want to be like me."

You begin to think materialistically. "The more I have, the more of a leader I will be." By trying to live up to what we see as society's standards, many of us grow up to be a materialistic follower, whether we intended to do so or not. You grow up believing that the accumulation of wealth very quickly transforms you into a great leader and endows you with great leadership qualities.

This way of thinking continues for generation after generation. Soon we have a world of "wannabees."

What do you think?

What kinds of wrong ideas about leadership do we get from observing society around us? What is the problem with seeing material things as a sign of leadership ability?

CHAPTER 4

POSSESSING A VISION

What constitutes a leader? What is a leader's "MO" (modus operandi, or "method of operating")? What are the qualities of a leader? Can I have them? Sure you can, but there are no A-B-C formulas for leadership. Leadership comes with all sorts of philosophies and lifestyles. No two leaders are made the same. What they share though, are some basic truths. As people develop into leaders, they enhance these truths to their satisfaction, and then establish fundamental principles.

Leaders must be able to have vision. They must be able to see what's going on, and then adapt. Leaders with a vision give their followers something to believe in, something to work toward. They give them something to identify with. When you talk to leaders about what they foresee in the future, their eyes should light up. It's because they all have a vision.

When I speak of vision, I'm thinking about certain fundamentals that are able to create excitement and motivate those who might aspire to follow you. These fundamentals include such things as:

- Inspiring loyalty and caring through the involvement of those you are leading.
- Clearly seeing and conveying the unique strengths, values, beliefs, and directions of your vision.

- Continuously communicating your vision to everyone involved.
- Inspiring enthusiasm and commitment in your vision.

Your values form the bases for everything that is going to take place as you go forth to lead. The people following you will make the decision early to trust you and to follow you when they recognize that you are what they are seeking in leadership. They will know if you share their values. If they will beg to differ with your values, they will go the other way because they do not, or choose not, to believe in the values you are laying down.

These values must be established early. Think of times when you "just went along with the plan" and later found yourself lowering your standards because you had been overwhelmed and taken in by the values of someone else leading you, when you should have been the leader.

Keep your vision clear. Keep your enthusiasm. Focus on your goals, and you will be fine.

Such was the case in my own coaching career. When I first became a head coach, I would sit and think about how I was going to win the state championship one day. And then I thought that after I won it, I would win it every year. My team was going to be the best ever. ... Then I met my team. At that time I had just been named head coach of the girls' basketball team. These girls had never won a basketball game before. Their school had just gone through six consecutive losing seasons. The last five seasons, they had not won a single game. So much for my dreams – I could almost see them going out the window.

Then it occurred to me: I am the team's leader. My vision is their vision. I must convince them that they can see what I see. I must keep them focused on my plans and goals for the team. That's what leaders do: they develop a plan, and they develop a vision. Through hard work, dedication, and a clear eye on the vision, my girls won their first-ever basketball game. This allowed the other coaches and me to convince the team that if they listened to and bought into our vision, they would be successful.

Leaders must begin with a vision, and be able to communicate that vision to others. Leaders must also possess other valuable qualities, some of which I will address in the next chapter. Remember that there are numerous things you can do to enhance your leadership skills, but in this book I'm showing you those fundamental qualities necessary as a foundation for successful leadership.

What do you think?

How would you define "vision" in leadership? What might be your vision for leadership?

CHAPTER 5

CHARACTERISTICS
OF LEADERSHIP

It is difficult to name all the principles that make a great leader. Some of the basic qualities of a leader are: good communication skills, articulate speech, ability to think on his or her feet, sense of humor, flexibility, integrity, a heart of servanthood, a compelling presence, and empathy. Having a lot of money and driving an expensive car are not prerequisites to be an outstanding leader. It's far deeper than just being good at your job.

You must have innovative thinking skills. You must be able to make a positive and inspiring impact on others. You must be able to motivate others. You need the ability to think and act "outside the box," beyond the norm. You should dare to be different – for all the right reasons. Innovation requires a certain amount of awareness as well as creativeness. A great strategy is this: Within your mind, you need to observe, then make the connection, and then analyze or figure out everything connected with your innovative thought. You must be willing to think broadly (outside the box). This usually will trigger another, synchronous event or action and, when this happens, your creative juices will begin to flow like crazy. You will find that somewhere within those seemingly "wild ideas" (innovation at its best), there will be valuable solutions to a lot of your problems or concerns. Leaders must have purpose and be able to express that purpose to others. This often takes courage.

Now if you think like me, the word "courage" may immediately bring to mind a picture of the Cowardly Lion in "The Wizard of Oz." So to help you think in other directions about courage, I have written down a few quotes about courage that you may or may not have heard. Recalling these quotes may help you when your courage is tested during your quest for successful leadership. Here are a few:

From Dale Carnegie: "Remember, today is the to-morrow you worried about yesterday."

From Eleanor Roosevelt: "No one can make you feel inferior without your consent."

Also from Eleanor Roosevelt: "You gain strength, courage, and confidence by every experience in which you look fear in the face. You must do the thing in which you think you cannot do."

From Abraham Lincoln: "It is difficult to make a man miserable while he feels worthy of himself, and claims kindred to the great God who made him."

From Henry David Thoreau: "Live your beliefs and you can turn the world around."

From Mark Twain: "Courage is the resistance to fear, mastery to fear – not absence to fear."

Courage is a great part of leadership. Keep in mind that I am helping you to identify characteristics and qualities necessary to becoming a successful leader, with outstanding leadership qualities.

Jeremiah 1:9-10 says: "Then the LORD reached

out his hand and touched my mouth and said to me, 'Now, I have put my words in your mouth. See, today I appoint you over nations and kingdoms to uproot and tear down, to destroy and overthrow, to build and to plant.'" When the Lord said this to Jeremiah, He was in essence saying, "I am creating in you a leader."

What I am trying to do is simply to help you become a leader through biblical principles in order to build the great foundation necessary to be successful.

History is replete with great leaders: George Washington, Napoleon, Sojourner Truth, Rosa Parks, Dr. Martin Luther King Jr., Rev. Billy Graham, to name a few. What separates these leaders from other people? Each of them had important values, and they stuck to their values, even in the face of great opposition.

Let's talk about values. Let's talk about how these leaders lived. What do we know about their lifestyles? Did people trust them?

Of course they did. ... Why? Because they walked with honor and integrity. They developed a trust with people, and they commanded respect wherever they went. Their inner character was on display in their daily walk.

Now, the Bible also records some great leaders, with great stories: Moses, Sampson, King Solomon, Queen Esther, Job, John the Baptist. But not one person, whether from the Bible or from history books, was a more perfect, more important, more qualified leader than Our Lord and Savior, Jesus Christ!

What do you think?

What does it mean to have courage in leadership? What kind of courage do you need to be a leader?

CHAPTER 6

PORTRAIT
OF A LEADER

What was it about Jesus? What made Him such a magnificent leader? Jesus had all the wealth of the Heavenly Father, but He never bragged about it. Yet people followed Him. In biblical times, a man with a lot of cattle, land, and servants was considered to be truly somebody, a man of standing. Jesus never had such worldly possessions. Jesus had no more than a handful of goods, primarily the clothes He wore. So why were people so drawn to Jesus as a leader?

Why did twelve men so quickly leave what they were doing so that they could follow Jesus and be His disciples? John's family owned their own business. Matthew was a well-known tax collector, a lucrative profession if not an honorable one. Some who were not among the chosen Twelve Apostles followed Jesus nonetheless. The rich man Zacchaeus was so drawn to Jesus that he climbed a sycamore tree just so he could see the Lord, and then repented of his sins. He gave back all the money he had taken by dishonest means, just to follow Jesus. What would make a man do something like that? Even some who had never met Jesus, men such as Luke the physician, gave up a great deal to follow Jesus.

Could it be that Jesus possessed the qualities we will be looking at, characteristics that make someone a true leader? If we could pattern our lives after

Jesus, would we become great leaders by following His example? Could Jesus possibly have given each one of us the same qualities He possessed so that we could be more like Him?

Here is a thought to ponder: Jesus didn't come to earth to be a leader, as we would expect a leader to be. On the contrary, He came to serve. However, through His serving He became a leader, one whose example of servant leadership was imitated by others, who in turn served a great many people. Jesus, as a servant, displayed great leadership qualities through His servanthood toward others. Here is what Jesus had to say about it:

"Suppose one of you had a servant plowing or looking after the sheep. Would he say to the servant when he comes in from the field, 'Come along now and sit down to eat'? Would he not rather say, 'Prepare my supper, get yourself ready and wait on me while I eat and drink; after that you may eat and drink'? Would he thank the servant because he did what he was told to do? So you also, when you have done everything you were told to do, should say, 'We are unworthy servants; we have only done our duty.' " (Luke 17:7-10)

That is what servanthood meant to Jesus. But what about us?

Sometimes I work as a substitute teacher in various classes at a private elementary school. One of the coolest awards given out at this school is called the "I am 3rd" award. One day I noticed that a little girl was wearing the "I am 3rd" medal, so I asked her if she knew what it meant. She was shy, and just smiled. So I told her what it meant: "It means ... Jesus 1st, others 2nd, and yourself 3rd." If she would look closely at the letters, I said, she would see that they spell "JOY." She beamed with delight. Joy is the reward for servanthood, I told her.

One time, one of my older brothers, William, gave me some money. The family had all gathered at his home for some occasion during the years when I was a young, broke college student. I was getting ready to leave when William asked if I needed anything. I said no, because I knew of his obligations to his family and his children. But William reached into his billfold, pulled out his last $50 bill, and handed it to me. That was all the money he had at the time. My other brothers balked and said, "You don't have to give that to him." William looked at them and said, "I know, but he's my baby brother, and whatever I have is his also." Wow! Everyone was quiet. Putting others ahead of yourself is true servanthood. (I love you, William! And all my family! Smile)

Be careful that you don't misinterpret servanthood, so you don't end up feeling empty, used, and abused. The focus of servanthood, as with anything else, must be on Jesus and our relationship with Him.

What do you think?

What did servanthood mean for Jesus? How does servanthood and our attitude toward serving affect our leadership?

CHAPTER 7

LEARNING TO FOCUS

Now know this: People will begin to expect too much from you; this is human nature. In turn, you will expect too much from them. Unrealistic expectations usually lead to major disappointments. That's why true leadership requires us to be extremely careful about our focus. In doing this, we can help to avoid the problem of unrealistic expectations that others place on us. When we focus on each other, rather than on Christ, we very easily slip into unrealistic expectations.

Our desire for others' gratitude can become insatiable. No amount of gratitude from others is enough. Nothing that anyone else can say or do will properly compensate you for your efforts to improve the human condition – so you start to think. When we serve people in order to receive their approval or their gratitude, we set up ourselves for hurt, disappointment, and even failure.

I know of this man who has a heart of gold. There isn't anything he wouldn't do for anyone. Oftentimes, he would rather go without than to see someone else suffer. I always believed this was a great spirit for my friend until people started taking advantage of him.

One favor turned into two, and two favors turned into four. After volunteering to pay a telephone bill, he was soon asked to pay a gas and electric bill. After paying the gas and electric bill, he was asked to make the house payment. Can you see the pattern here?

You can't possibly satisfy everyone when all they want is more, more, more.

Now, check this out. It appears that my friend was being easily taken advantage of because of his "great heart," right? Well, read on. I found out later that my friend had a plan. He wasn't truly giving from his heart – at least in the sense that I thought. He had an ulterior motive. He was trying to get the girl that belonged to the phone bill, the gas bill, the electric bill, and the house note. And when things didn't work out, my friend was left feeling used and abused. Why was this? Because he was doing these things for all the wrong reasons. (He has now learned, and loves God!)

Now you might say, "Aw, Coach D, that happens all the time. Guys always want to please girls, and girls always want to please guys, so they do crazy things." But other people tried to take advantage of him as well. This type of treatment caused my friend to start feeling cold, hard, and very cautious when it came to doing for others.

Why am I telling you this? I'm telling you because when you do things for others only when it can benefit yourself, you leave the door open for hurt, rejection, disappointment, and even failure.

A good leader must be aware of this. Just when things seem to be going great, when you start to feel good about what you are doing for other people, they begin to expect more. It seems their cup is never full. You begin to sour on the idea of service. The same is true when you start to expect too much from others.

Listen, the main point here is that if you have already developed a solid personal relationship with Christ, your focus will be on serving Him and gaining His approval, not on human beings and their fickle needs. My friend, when you are totally absorbed in Jesus Christ and in pleasing Him, you will find that everything you do – including service to others – will be out of response to Him and in accordance with His will.

We do not serve man; we serve God alone. We help others by means of the love of God that He has put in us. Don't look for the approval of man; instead, seek the approval of God! When you do, the true meaning of servanthood comes out, and your leadership qualities are enhanced. (Isn't it interesting that I talk to you about leadership and servanthood in the same breath? It's because leadership is not just something you have, but something you do – beginning with servanthood.)

Once you get past your own ego and stop believing people who tell you that "you are all that"; once you stop thinking that you have earned the right to be heard and that you deserve to have others listen; once you humble yourself and see what it really means to lead (which is to serve) – only then will your inner light shine through.

At that point you will have an overwhelming desire

to serve, and to do so unconditionally. You won't have an expectation of receiving something in return. You will do it unconditionally because Christ lives inside you. Christ will be working through you, reaching out to others for the sake of His Kingdom. When you do it right – when Christ is your main focus – then people will want to emulate you, and you will begin to see how awesome it is to be a leader. Building for Christ's Kingdom is what servanthood is truly about.

Does mastery of this make you a leader? No. However, it is the groundbreaking for building you into a dynamic leader with outstanding leadership qualities. It is the beginning.

This is your foundation. When you learn about servanthood and begin to serve, everything else will fall into place and start to make sense. Let's move on.

What do you think?

What does it mean to have "focus" in leadership? How can we focus on what is important about leadership?

CHAPTER 8

WALKING IN
INTEGRITY

Now, as Jesus was demonstrating servanthood, He was walking the walk and talking the talk. His integrity was an inspiration for those around Him.

Jesus once was challenged as to the truthfulness of His claims to be God Incarnate. "Jesus replied, 'If I glorify myself, my glory means nothing. My Father, whom you claim as your God, is the one who glorifies me. Though you do not know him, I know him. If I said I did not, I would be a liar like you, but I do know him and keep his word.'" (John 8:54-55)

It was vital for Jesus to maintain His integrity, to always tell the truth no matter what challenges might come. What is your definition of integrity? Integrity is soundness. Integrity is firm adherence to a code or standard of values, especially when it is not to your own profit. Do you show integrity with all your friends? Or, do you just practice it when it is convenient, with your "church friends" (the ones you see only on Sundays). When you have to choose between what's right and what's advantageous to you, do you always do what is right? Are you willing to place integrity at the top of your list when you plan your steps to successful leadership?

Is your word your bond? Can people count on you? Do people believe in you? The Bible tells us to let our "yes" be a "yes," and let our "no" be a "no." In other words, mean what you say, and stick to it. Be honest and sincere, and your integrity will shine!

I was watching a basketball practice from a distance one day. Unexpectedly, the coach was called out for a meeting. I was watching because I was applying for an assistant coaching position there at the time, and wanted to see what the girls would do if there were no coaches around. I wanted to see if they had enough loyalty to cause their integrity to shine through.

Well, you guessed it. They began playing around and joking with each other. No drills were being done. I knew from experience that they had work to do, even if the coach wasn't there. Well, no work was being done, and no drills were being run. I watched this for a while, and then noticed that one girl left the group and went to the other end of the gym, and began doing drills. Hmmm, I thought. This went on for a while. The other girls kept joking around as if not caring about her or what they were supposed to be doing, while the one young lady just kept right on working.

Soon, another player left the group to go down to the other end and start doing drills. Then, a couple more did the same. Soon, all the laughing and joking stopped, and the girls all began doing their drills.

When the coach returned, he was pleased, because he knew he could trust the one player to do what was right. Because she did, others followed. That's leadership with integrity. The coach knew he had a good leader in her, and now I had seen it too.

Can you be trusted to do the right thing even when no one is around? Are you motivated only by what is popular? Think about your answers. Think about the last time you were in a situation in which you let popularity overrule what you knew was right. (Am I getting close to where you live? Are you still thinking your leadership skills are beyond question?)

Rev. Brian Kinney, a friend of mine, tells about a college fraternity brother of his who had the opportunity to avoid responsibility for a traffic accident. The fraternity brother, named Tom, was driving with several friends in his convertible when he saw a traffic light turning yellow just in time to slam on the brakes and skid to a stop, part-way in the intersection. So Tom threw the transmission into reverse and, without looking, backed his car right into the front of a car stopped behind him. Soon a police officer was on the scene, and people started saying that it was the other driver's fault, that Tom had stopped for the light and the other driver had hit the back of Tom's car. The officer even started to write a ticket to the poor man who was driving the car behind Tom. But something in Tom – something called "integrity" – wouldn't let him go along. He went to the officer and admitted that it was he who was at fault.

Have you ever heard someone say, "He has good morals," or, "She has good morals?"

Do you know what morals are? The word "morals"

comes from the Latin "moralis." It means: "of or concerned with the principles of right and wrong in relation to human character."

When you have integrity, you have morals. You have a foundation that is solid and reliable. No matter what happens in the world, no matter what people throw at you, your heart's desire is to know God better and to please Him more. You will do the right thing. That's walking with integrity.

Integrity begins in the heart. A pure heart is part of the foundation of leadership. "So as the heart" – "so as the man." When Jesus said, "Blessed are the pure in heart" (Matthew 5:8), I believe He meant the heart as the core of our very beings.

The heart is the center of all desires, thoughts, perceptions, imaginations, intentions, reasoning, purpose, will, and faith. Proverbs 4:23 tells us "to guard your heart, for it is the wellspring of life." The heart is the central meeting place for all your emotions, prejudices, and wisdom. People tell us to "speak to me from your heart" because they know the heart is the true you. The heart is where everything comes together.

Within the heart are two paths: one of them is the route into your heart, and the other is the road leading out. The one entering the heart is what determines your focus. The things you dwell on create intentions and reasoning. The heart is the center point of your spiritual life. If your heart allows evil inside, you will become evil. If your heart is filled with good things – love, peace, and joy – then you will be good.

In the end ... you will follow your heart ... I promise you!

Jesus said, "Blessed are the pure in heart, for they shall see God." Listen, my friend: if you want to draw closer to God, search yourself. Get rid of the clutter, and get rid of the junk in your heart. Purify it! Send it packing on the road that leads out of the heart. When all that mess is cleaned out, you'll see God in there. You may not have been able to see Him for the clutter, but He never left you. He has always been there, but you allowed things to cover Him up. God loves you! Keep a clean heart. Being a leader means having a leader's heart, clean and pure.

If you have harbored anything in your heart that you wouldn't want exposed to anybody and everybody, then it's time to replace it with what would be pleasing to God. As the Apostle Paul wrote, " ... whatever is true, whatever is noble, whatever is right, whatever is pure, whatever is lovely, whatever is admirable — if anything is excellent or praiseworthy — think about such things." (Philippians 4:8)

If you keep junk in your heart, out of your heart will come junk. Jesus said, "The good man brings good things out of the good stored up in his heart, and the evil man brings evil things out of the evil stored up in his heart. For out of the overflow of his heart his mouth speaks." (Luke 6:45)

What do you think?

What does it mean to you to have integrity? In what areas of life is it most difficult to maintain integrity?

CHAPTER 9

SPIRITUAL DEPTH

Becoming a man or woman with leadership qualities requires us to develop spiritual depth. It is easier to stay focused during the tough times if you already have created a fundamental base before the hard times come. Believe me, there will be tough times. Your foundational principles will prepare you to know what to do during tough times, and they will help see you through difficulties. Strong leadership is about moving forward when faced with heartbreak and disappointment. Leaders must sometimes put aside their own feelings for the sake of perspective.

Some time back, I applied for the position of head basketball coach at a particular school. I had been the assistant basketball coach there for quite a while, and now the head coach was retiring. Everyone around the school and the league assured me it was a "no-brainer." They all thought that I would be named the coach's successor. Even I believed it. I began making plans as to what I was going to do when I did get the job. I began preparing myself. Then the announcement of the new coach came. It was not me. The school had chosen someone else. "How could they?" I thought, "I was the man! I was the choice!" Fire burned inside me, and I was not a happy camper.

Many of the parents had questions about the decision. Some of the players wanted to quit. Other

coaches on the staff didn't want to coach anymore.
Everyone was turning to me for a response. We had
a problem, and I wasn't feeling much like a humble
servant. I, and it seemed a thousand others in town,
thought that the school had picked the worst candi-
date. How vain for me to think like that!

Now understand this: I knew everyone liked and
respected me. It seemed that no one liked or respected the new coach. I had a decision to make. If I pouted
and quit (things that I seemed to love to do in my early years – well, maybe not quit, but I sure did pout), I
knew others would follow. A whole lot of others were
loyal friends and teammates, and I knew they would
support me. Despite my own feelings, I knew that
for the sake of the school and the athletic program,
I had to swallow my pride and show true leadership
by staying. So I did, and everyone else did too. We
gathered around the new coach and, although it was
tough in the beginning, we came through.

I'm glad I took that route despite my own disappointment and hurts. It was the right thing to do. It
is important to show others the meaning of leadership when disappointments and heartaches fill your
spirit. I think that I am a better leader today because
of that sort of decision.

Another important quality of leadership is that a
leader must not be afraid to make a mistake. Have
you ever made a mistake? Have you ever done something you wish you hadn't, but knew you had to go
forward and face the music? I've done that more than

once, and I probably will make even more mistakes after this book is written; in fact, I'm sure I will. You see, I'm not afraid to make mistakes, because I know that's how you learn, that's how you grow. As a coach, it happens to me all the time. Coaches aren't perfect, and neither are you. You must be willing to take a risk.

During an intense game against a great rival, our best point guard pulled down a rebound with 5 seconds on the clock. We were down 1 point. She was fast, I mean really fast. And she could handle the ball. She headed down court. I saw the other team hustle back to cut her off, and I panicked. (Never let them see you sweat!) Frantically I yelled, "Time out! Time out!" just as my little point guard shot the ball. Yep, you guessed it. "swish," nothing but net!

The shot went in. But ... it was ruled "no good" because it came after I had called and was granted the time out. The crowd went crazy. The point guard looked at me, and I looked at her, and I knew what she must have been thinking. I felt it too. We went back on the floor, and we lost! I felt miserable, but I had to go and face the team. I did just that, because I knew they trusted me. They believed in me to make the right judgment. So I told them very frankly that I should not have called time out. We had the perfect scenario. We had the player I wanted with the ball, and she was doing what she did best. I couldn't have asked for a better situation. But we lost, and now we would move on! I was honest, I was upfront with them, and they respected that.

When a leader does make a mistake, he must move on from that point. Everyone makes mistakes at some time or another. Some mistakes are big, some are small. Some people's mistakes affect no one but themselves; others' mistakes affect a great many people. We all make them. A good leader needs to recognize those mistakes and pray, repent, and move on.

What do you think?

What does it mean to have spiritual depth? How should you deal with those times that you make mistakes?

CHAPTER 10

FACING JEALOUSY AND ENVY

B e prepared, though, for leadership qualities to make you a "big splash" in your neighborhood. Was Jesus a big splash in His community? You betcha! That's why He aroused curiosity in so many people. That's why jealousy against Him was so rampant. You see, Jesus was no fake. He would take people who thought they were good, and expose their inner lives. On the outside they looked good, they talked well and used high-class words; they had fancy clothes, and they did all the right rituals. They tried desperately to camouflage what was going on inside. These were the "wannabees" of Jesus' time.

Really, though, these people were without direction, longing for status, wanting to be "someone." Jesus saw through all of this. He exposed their inner beings, though in a gentle way that offered grace and mercy. People were drawn to Jesus because of His leadership qualities – integrity, servanthood, humility, respect, and grace, to name a few. People sensed an overwhelming safety in being transparent with Jesus. Instead of ridiculing them and piling shame upon them, as others did, Jesus offered compassion, grace, and mercy. How cool is that!

What is the point of me saying all this? Why am I trying to tell you so much about Jesus, when I started out to write about leadership? Hello! ... Because Jesus IS leadership! Jesus displayed great leadership qualities so that they would be emulated by His disciples, who in turn would go out and lead others. Good leadership builds character and self-worth. When leadership is taught correctly, it will inspire others to become leaders. Inspiration is the fruit of good leadership.

True leadership will be attacked often with jealousy, envy, and all sorts of criticism. "Wannabees" will be jealous of you. When you go against the flow, as leaders sometimes must, critics will find you. Rest assured of that. But why?

Others want to figure out why you are special. They want to know why people are drawn to you. They want to know why people follow you. Secretly, they want to be like you. Jesus had many critics, including the Pharisees. The Pharisees wanted to be like Jesus; however, they didn't want to change their ways. Instead, they attacked Jesus' leadership qualities at every opportunity, and tried to bring Him down to their level. They were talking the talk, but Jesus was walking the walk.

What do you think?

Why do people become jealous over one another's standing? What can you do when you are tempted to become jealous? What about those who become jealous of you?

CHAPTER 11

COMMUNICATION ... GETTING THE MESSAGE ACROSS

Let's talk about some basics of leadership. One of the most basic issues is communication. How important is communication?

Being a coach, I always thought that I could talk with anyone. I believed I could get my message across to anyone who needed to hear it. You could put me in a room with any group, and I always thought that I could communicate with that group.

And then ... I got married.

When I was first married, my wife would always talk with me about communication. She would say to me, "We need to talk more; we need to communicate." I thought to myself, "How can she say this? – I talk to her all the time! I'm constantly telling her about my team, whichever one I'm coaching at the time. I even give her 'play-by-play.' How could she possibly say, 'We need to talk more,' or 'We need to communicate.'?"

Well, communication is certainly more than just talking. It's more than an "all about you" conversation. It's about listening. It's about understanding other persons' feelings.

It's being able to translate feelings into words. What my wife was trying to tell me was that, yes, we talk – but I needed to learn to listen. We needed to learn to communicate. We needed to recognize and understand each other.

Leaders must have the ability to communicate, verbally and nonverbally. To communicate as a great leader, you must be an active listener as well as a good talker.

Another part of communication is our "walk." A person's "walk" is usually more important than his or her "talk." When most people think about good communication, they immediately think about being a great speaker, someone who talks a lot. True, you do need a certain manner of speech, but it is your daily way of life that catches the attention of others. Someone whose life speaks loudly before he opens his mouth is a "silent communicator." If you are such a "silent communicator," people are likely to follow you and to trust you.

If you walk with integrity, you will convey a message of trust, honor, and self-worth. These are all great attributes of leadership. When your message is misconstrued because of your own disloyalty, undependability, or lack of integrity, your leadership will take a severe nosedive. Be careful to convey the right message, the one you want to get across. Sending mixed messages or wrong messages will wreak havoc on the communication you are trying to achieve. Be very careful not to lead a double life. Follow a life of integrity. Be honorable. It's never too late to begin. It may be difficult to turn around people's perception of you, but it can be done – starting now.

What do you think?

Why is communication so important in leadership? What are some things that get in the way of communication? How can you deal with these obstacles?

CHAPTER 12

THE ART OF ARTICULATION

A rticulation is another important quality for leadership. Society has determined that you must be articulate in order to be a good leader. What is articulation? If my "walk" is my voice, why do I need articulation skills? You need articulation skills because as you grow in leadership, there will be times when your voice will need to be heard. When it does, your voice will need to command respect. If your "walk" is right, your voice can enhance the trust people already have in you.

Articulation is the ability to express yourself in a way that displays confidence, knowledge, and professionalism. It means you are skilled in your speech. Ever since I was a little boy, I've been impressed with big words and great speech. One of my older brothers, Donald, would always make it a point to work on his speech and his vocabulary. Don was always the guy using big words, at school or at home. He would use words that most people can't spell, and don't know their meanings. Anyway, Don would take the utmost pride in his ability with the language. One day I overheard Donald engaged in a conversation. My ears caught Don using those big words again. I was feeling ornery, as I sometimes did. So, I just interrupted him and flat-out asked, "OK, Donald, just what do those words mean anyway?" I was secretly hoping to catch him off-guard. Well, without missing a beat, Don explained the words and their meanings. Then he picked up where he had left off with his conversation and used even bigger words and phrases than before. Wow, what a guy!

Normally I would have been embarrassed that my little joke had backfired, but this time I wasn't. I was amazed. I was so impressed that I started asking Don to teach me those words and to help me expand my vocabulary. As I learned new words and phrases, my level of confidence began to rise to a point few could match. I felt good about myself. I knew that I could speak knowledgeably and confidently to anybody and about anything. I felt that my world had been elevated to a level usually reserved for theologians, philosophers, and the sort.

Articulation isn't all about using big words, but it helps greatly to have confidence with words. Your voice speaks louder if you are able to plan your speech carefully and wisely. I was able to gain confidence because I dared to take the challenge to be the best that I could be, inside and out. You can sugar-coat it all you want on the outside, but if you don't have the "right" things going on inside, the real you will surface eventually. If your goal is to lead and to inspire, you need to develop the skills necessary to speak clearly and to speak well. Keep it real. Do what you need to do to improve your voice and your articulation.

Today I am able to adapt to any level of communication, and I can do it with the utmost confidence.

Being a coach means that you must communicate with players, parents, and the public – and you never know at what level of intellect you will have to communicate. So, as the Boy Scouts say, "Be Prepared."

What do you think?

What does it mean to you to be articulate? Why is this important in leadership? In what ways can you prepare yourself to be articulate?

CHAPTER 13

PROBLEM SOLVING

An enjoyable part of leadership is the ability to think on your feet. You must learn to solve problems quickly and confidently. Take my brother-in-law, Spencer, now he is a leader. There are plenty of great leaders among my family members, but I want particularly to mention Spencer. He has that quick-witted ability to think on his feet. Spence has a God-given talent to assess a situation, calculate a decision and then confident enough to present his answer with great articulation. Spence is a great man of God and bases his responses on integrity...his daily walk. Because of this, Spence is not afraid to make a call, a decision. For that I give him much love.

Sometimes I think he's border-line genius because he is so quick with his responses.

What a great guy! Being able to recognize assess and react, wow!! You can't be afraid to take risks. Spence, I love you, man! Keep doing what you are doing -- you're planting the seeds. A lot of times, no one else wants to decide. No one else steps up to the plate. Most people are naturally afraid, usually out of fear. They tend to sit back and do nothing. Spence is a leader. Leaders take charge. They don't just sit back and watch. They do it!

This challenges you to keep sharp. Right or wrong, you must be willing to take risks and make decisions.

There are times when you must choose a course of action according to your beliefs, based on what you think is the right thing to do. You have to step out of your comfort zone. This may sound simple, but it isn't always that way in practice. It is an important part of being a leader.

Sometimes there is no perfect answer. Nobody is going to get everything he wants, all of the time. And you must not always make the decision that would benefit you the most. One time I was coaching basketball, and we had only one gym. The basketball team came to practice, and we discovered that the athletic department had scheduled two other teams plus the band for the gym at the same time as our practice. There was no way to share the gym with all these groups! Even though other staff members were there, everyone was looking to me for guidance. "What do I do?" I thought. This situation had plenty of potential for ill will – we were always struggling for gym time. So I quickly gathered my team and had them watch a game film of our next opponent. Then I coordinated the other two teams in a scrimmage, and suggested that the band use the time as if it were an actual game – to practice while the teams were playing. This may not have been the best possible decision, but a decision had to be made. There wasn't time to debate all the options. That's what leaders do. They think on their feet, quickly, logically, and confidently. Never let the others see you sweat!

Sometimes the best decision is to leave matters

as they are. This was not one of those times, though. The old me would've wanted to pass the buck and tell the others, "Call the athletic director – it's his problem; let him figure it out." I'm so glad that I had matured in leadership by then so I would not sink to that level.

All of this comes under the umbrella of "perspective" – being able to see the big picture, to make sound decisions and not take a lot of time doing so. The ability to think on your feet will help greatly when you face tough decisions. Your decisions may not always be the most popular, but they are decisions that you must make with confidence. Sometimes ANY decision is better than no decision.

Trust yourself to do the right thing. Believe in yourself!

What do you think?

In what kinds of situations do you need to think quickly "on your feet"? What does "Sometimes ANY decision is better than no decision" mean?

CHAPTER 14

LAUGHING OUT LOUD

Humor is a part of leadership. Everyone likes a good laugh, and leaders are in a position to provide that laugh. Pastor Tim (one of my brothers-in-law) is a perfectionist. He has a knack for making sure everything is just right. E-V-E-R-Y-T-H-I-N-G! He can almost tell you how many drops of gasoline are left in his car's tank, even though the gauge may be reading "empty." You gotta love him – he's awesome!

Sometimes as Tim preaches, he fidgets with some of the things on the pulpit. If his notes are crooked, he straightens them. If his Bible is upside-down, he turns it right-side up. He's a perfectionist. This can be good, but he does these things constantly. How many times can you move a Bible during a sermon? Tim keeps doing these things almost like a nervous twitch. (Now I know my brother-in-law is not nervous about anything. he's 6 feet 6 inches tall, and two hundred and ... uh, well, let's just say 6 feet 6 inches tall.) However, to us in the pews, it does appear that he is nervous. He likes things to be just right.

Anyway, the church's youth pastor, decided for a church dinner to imitate Pastor Tim when he was called upon to speak. P.W. (Pastor Will) had Pastor Tim down pat. He moved about, "twidged and fidged," moved his Bible and notes about a hundred times, and had everyone just roaring with laughter, including Pastor Tim.

Leaders must be willing not only to provide laughs when tensions run high, but also to laugh with the troops. Being able to recognize humor and seize the moment is a great leadership quality. One way others learn to respect you is to perceive you to be "real."

Now, I've never been terribly good at telling jokes, but I have attempted a few, though usually, I goof them up. When I get to the punch line, it never is as funny as when it was told to me. A lot of people already know I am horrible at telling jokes, so they begin laughing not so much at the joke, but at me telling the joke. So everyone has fun and we all are able to relax. This can help build a special trust. Leaders will be accepted and trusted more when their followers see their human side.

Twenty-some years ago, when the Rev. Harry Long was pastoring little Sycamore Presbyterian Church in Midlothian, Virginia, he was presiding over the Lord's Supper and was breaking the loaf of communion bread as he said, "This is my body, broken for you." At just that moment, the loaf broke apart by itself, and part of it hit the table and then the floor, rolling for several feet before it came to rest right in front of two little boys who tried their best to stifle their laughter. Rev. Long, who was fairly young at the time, at first looked embarrassed as he saw that the rest of the congregation too, was trying its best not to laugh. Finally, he said, "OK, let's all take a minute to get our laughs out, and then go on." So the congregation laughed a few moments, then settled back into the seriousness of the sacrament. The young pastor was able to laugh at himself, the congregation was able to see his human side, and the whole incident became one of those golden memories as the church grew and matured.

Laughing is a great activity. It is also proven scientifically to help relieve stress. Good humor offers help in making decisions. If you have the ability to laugh even when things go wrong, you will not be worried about making mistakes. This can relieve the stress of a high-pressure situation. As far as I know, a good laugh has never hurt anyone. Go ahead ... laugh a little! It's OK ... I promise!

What do you think?

How does it help to have a sense of humor about your-self? Are you ever sensitive about anyone laughing at you? How could you handle such a situation?

CHAPTER 15

KNOW THYSELF

Moving along in the list of leadership qualities, we come to flexibility. Being flexible – the ability to adapt to different people and situations – is a powerful tool in leadership. No two people are the same. Looks, mannerisms, and speech may be alike, but the intellect is unique. God created each of us with a one-of-a-kind mind. We may pattern after other people, but our minds do not come from the same mold.

Dr. David Calhoun, professor at Covenant Theological Seminary in St. Louis, tells about the time he was invited to preach at a church in Jamaica. Dr. Calhoun's sermons normally ran about 30 minutes, and so after he preached those 30 minutes, he sat down. However, Jamaican sermons typically run longer – sometimes an hour or more. After Dr. Calhoun sat down, nobody else got up to do anything in the service. After an awkward pause, someone else on the platform whispered to him, "They haven't heard enough. They want you to preach some more!" Dr. Calhoun whispered back, "I only brought the one sermon. I don't have anything else to preach." So the Jamaican said, "Get up and preach it again!" So Dr. Calhoun got up and preached the same sermon over again, and the Jamaicans were satisfied, and the service moved ahead. Dr. Calhoun just had to adjust to the Jamaicans' different way of thinking.

Flexibility in decision-making offers a variety of choices for any given situation. When you are flexible, you are more willing to look at the whole picture, and from other points of view. When we are flexible, we can make changes as needed.

Now, don't misuse your flexibility. There are times when you as a leader must stand your ground. In my younger days, I made a bad decision concerning my school work. I didn't commit myself to it as much as I should have. I played around, did what I wanted to do, and didn't give "two flips" about school. Well, guess what, I became ineligible to participate in sports. I played all sports, and this was track season and we were having a track meet. I was fast, I was quick, I was good, and I wanted to compete. But my coach said "No." He was doing the right thing, though the policy wasn't written in stone – so I thought, anyway.

I begged and pleaded. I pleaded and begged. I kicked and screamed. I had friends and family members coming to watch the meet, even my girlfriend. Why hadn't someone told me this would happen? It couldn't have been my fault. I should be allowed to compete. I would do better next time. I promised everything, including the moon. My coach held his ground, and said "No."

I know that my coach could have allowed me to compete, but what would that have taught me? Today I am thankful to that coach, Kevin Rose, for teaching me an important lesson, even though it placed our team in a situation to lose a big meet. A lesson was being learned, and a lesson was being taught.

I am glad Coach Rose made the decision not to be flexible. His willingness to stand his ground helped to mature me in that important aspect of leadership. Today, I can teach the same to others. Believe in what you say. Believe in what you do. You must always stand up for what you believe is the right choice. However, there are gray areas for which flexibility is a must. True leaders learn to differentiate between times to be flexible, and times to stand their ground. As you grow into leadership, this will become second nature to you. You will have the skills to differentiate quickly. This comes with knowing people, and knowing yourself.

What do you think?

What does it mean to "know yourself"? Are there areas in which you are not flexible enough? Or areas in which you are too flexible?

CHAPTER 16

COMMANDING
PRESENCE

Now, let's consider your presence as a tool for leadership. How important is it? When you walk into a room, what happens? Do you carry a presence that says you are confident to be there? That you belong there? Or, is your presence saying, "Help, get me out of here quick!"?

Leadership demands a compelling presence. You must be able to convey to others that you are confident and secure in your decision-making. I remember doing some college recruiting and listening to several people saying how "professional" I looked and acted. One director told me, "Something happens whenever you are in a room – a glow comes over the room." Am I telling you this to give myself "high-fives?" No! I'm telling you this because people do notice whether or not someone has a presence. As frightened and nervous as I was at times, I still pulled myself together to display a confidence that they saw in my presence alone, before I said a word. That's "commanding presence." And you can have such a presence!

Now, do I mean that you need expensive clothing and high-profile jewelry? No, but you should wear the right clothes for each situation. I shop at the same stores where you shop; I buy the same clothes you buy – well, for the most part! I have always believed that the man makes the clothes – but use strategy when dressing.

My nephew, Keenan, recently graduated from Tennessee State University. Keenan is about 6-foot-5, and 155 lbs. That, my friend, is thin. But Keenan loves to shop for clothes that are five times too big for him. He says, "It's the cool, college way."

Keenan graduated from TSU with a degree in economics and finance, and he is working hard to find a position in business. Even though Keenan is sharp-witted, when he was getting ready for an interview he wore an outfit that not only was too big for him, but it also got in the way of his movement. Listen up! I can assure you that this "baggy clothes syndrome" that's cool for college is definitely NOT happening in the business world! I have a brother Robb who is 6-foot-9 and weighs about 420 lbs., and Keenan's clothes would almost be a little big on him. Ironically, Keenan loves to shop at the same stores as Robb. There definitely is something wrong with that picture, but we'll move on.

Most of Keenan's morning was spent trying to keep his pants from falling off!

Did Keenan give the air of a commanding presence? Did he attract positive attention? When potential employers saw him for the first time, they didn't exactly say, "Let's hire this guy – he commands respect."

What Keenan should have done was to assess his situation and make a decision that was appropriate to the environment he was entering. A little adjustment in his wardrobe could have made a world of difference in how he was perceived. Are you getting this? This is an important factor you need to know.

The way you walk, your approach, the words you use, all of these tell a story about you. You need to make sure that people are reading the book (you) the way you would want it written. Give that first impression a boost by having a compelling presence. Make sure that people know you care about the way you look. Trust me. If you care about the "little things," such as your appearance and the way you speak, people will believe that you care even more about the larger things and, ultimately, care about them.

Isn't that what we want? We want others to believe in us, to trust us, to believe we have the confidence to lead. Your attention to detail will make them believe you will take all things into consideration when making decisions. They will believe that you care, and people do follow leaders who care.

What do you think?

What does it mean to have a commanding presence? How could you have a more commanding presence around people? How could this help you in leadership?

CHAPTER 17

UNDERSTANDING
PEOPLE

Qualities of caring are vital for leaders, qualities such as empathy and compassion. It is essential that you care. You should feel the excitement, the joy, the pain of other people. Leaders understand the struggles of others and relate to them. You may not have experienced the exact same struggle, but you know enough about struggle in general. People sometimes confuse empathy and compassion with servanthood. Both of these deal with genuine care for others, but servanthood takes the idea to another level, to the point where you place the interests of others above your own.

Empathy and compassion are milestones on the way to servanthood, and the person who is empathetic and compassionate is well on his way toward servanthood.

The American Heritage Dictionary of the English Language defines "empathy" as "understanding so intimate that the feelings, thoughts, and motives of one, are readily comprehended by another." BINGO! That's it – being able to understand to the point that, even if you haven't been in the exact situation of another, you feel as though you have. What a great quality for a leader! Have you ever heard someone say, "I know how he feels. I know what he is going through," or, "I feel for you." If the person making that comment is being truthful, he is showing empathy.

Perhaps you have heard a story of compassion involving two rich men and a homeless man. The first rich man was walking down the street in the midst of a winter storm. Prepared for the cold in his long coat, hat, and gloves, he came across a homeless man sitting in a corner and trying to stay warm. The homeless man stood up and approached the rich man and said, "Sir, if I could only have some spare change to get something to eat, I would be so grateful." The rich man looked at the homeless man standing there with no coat or hat, and with tiny icicles forming under his nose. The rich man felt compassion and opened his billfold to offer a dollar. As he looked into his billfold, he saw that he had a hundred-dollar bill, two fifties, one twenty, and one ten. So he told the homeless guy, "I don't have any ones. I only have big bills, and I can't give you that much, but I will pray for you." Then he went on his way.

The second rich man came along and saw the same homeless man. The second rich man was dressed for the cold, too. As he saw the homeless man, he stopped and, without saying a word, he removed his warm Armani cashmere coat and put it on the homeless man. He did the same with his gloves and hat. Then the rich man reached into his pocket and pulled out his billfold. Inside, he had a fifty-dollar bill, two twenties, a ten and a one-dollar bill. The rich man took all the bills and gave them to the homeless man. He then smiled and began praying for the homeless man on the spot. Slowly, he walked away.

A group of college students had been nearby, observing the encounters with both rich men. They were so filled with compassion from the actions of the second rich man that they, too, began removing their coats, hats, and gloves, and giving to all of the homeless there. Down the street, as the second rich man was about to get into a car, he looked back, saw what was happening, and smiled. He knew that he had done the right thing.

The leadership of one man stepping forth and showing compassion prompted others to follow suit. As leaders, sometimes we allow our hearts to lead us the extra mile, in spite of what others may see as too much of a bother, something for which they didn't have the time or the interest.

Now, what about empathy? Empathy is not a hindrance, but rather another important piece of the puzzle of leadership. While you as a leader must be able to make sound decisions, empathy is a quality that helps you to see more clearly how to make those decisions. If you can demonstrate empathy in making decisions, others will see that you have the heart to be a human leader. They will trust your judgment more, and be more willing to follow you because they understand more about your character, more about why you decide as you do.

Growing up in a family of 12 kids, I had a lot of opportunities to see how things were done. Good or bad, right or wrong, I was able to see how things happened. As I became older, I was able to see reactions to those things, how people responded to certain decisions. I was able to start understanding "why" and "why not." This was a major part of gaining wisdom for leadership. And I'm proud of that. If every youth would pay closer attention to things around him as he is growing up, he will learn to discern qualities of leadership. It doesn't necessarily take a family of 12 kids to make this happen either. But, I must stress, through it all, open the Bible. Read God's Word!

Jesus Is Life!

Choose Life or Death

Life is Jesus Christ

Death is Satan.

What do you think?

What are empathy and compassion? What do they have to do with leadership?

CHAPTER 18

IT'S ALL A PROCESS – BEGIN WITH YOURSELF

Tomorrow's world needs leaders with sound integrity. It needs people like you, as you grow in becoming a leader. My job, and the job of other leaders, is to raise up others today for leadership tomorrow. My prayer is that you will understand how important it is to grasp securely the foundational principles from this book. As you learn and practice these principles, you will in turn be able to teach others. If we as leaders don't specialize in what we are doing, then there is no future in leadership. The world will be populated only with "wannabees."

In conclusion, let me remind you that leadership is a process. Don't be content with the way you are. As challenges arise, have the guts to go for it. Practice will keep you sharp. Look forward to new challenges and new situations. Leaders don't make excuses. This was drilled into my head over and over as a child, and now I pass it along to you. Don't make excuses either!

As I have heard it said, "Excuses are nothing but tools of the incompetent, who build monuments of nothingness, and those who specialize in their use seldom amount to anything in the pyramid of success." Be creative in your thinking. Learn to look in the mirror and like what you see. Stop being disappointed because you are not like another man or another woman.

Be yourself! Enhance the qualities within you, and others will emulate you. There is no need to be a "wannabee" – you can be a leader.

Remember the story of David in the Bible? He was a small shepherd boy, the youngest in his family. Nevertheless, David was called by God to serve His people. Through servanthood, David became a leader, king of Israel.

Know this: God calls all of us to serve, and through servanthood we display leadership.

At the beginning of this book we looked at foundational principles. Foremost among these principles is that of servanthood, and it is the rock-solid platform on which you should build. If servanthood is your foundation, then the other qualities of leadership will have strong roots.

God doesn't make mistakes. What God does is to give us the ability to choose the right rather than the wrong. David failed at times, as do all leaders. The only people not making mistakes are those who aren't doing anything at all. But you, like David, can repent, ask God for forgiveness, and move on. That is the way to deal with mistakes. Stay strong. Believe in yourself. Trust God.

Be true, because you never know who is watching. You never know whose life you are touching. Do unto others as you would have them do unto you. Love your neighbor as you love yourself. Love unconditionally.

Set the bar high. Leave the "wannabee" image behind. Step out into true leadership. Begin with true servanthood. Walk with integrity. Begin your tomorrow ... today! Be the best you can be. Do the best you can do. Do it for JESUS CHRIST! He is the Greatest Leader Man Has Ever Known. When you do this, you won't have to tell others that you are a leader. They will know, just by being in your presence. Amen!

What do you think?

In what ways is leadership a process? What kinds of steps are in that process? How can you become a better leader?

During preparation for this book, I have been thankful so many times to be inspired by the Bible, the Word of God. Other than the Bible, my favorite resource book, and one from which I've gained great wisdom and knowledge, is Max Lucado's devotional Bible, Experiencing the Heart of Jesus.

There are many more articles, books, and opinions out there concerning leadership, and I've read quite a few. However, I wanted those whose lives I contact and to whom I am accountable in my leadership walk to know the principles for which I stand.

My prayer is that through this book, as well as my daily walk, the youth and potential leaders that I know will grow up to emulate a lifestyle that is Christ-like in every way possible! And for this, God deserves ALL THE GLORY!

This book is a message to you … from my heart!!! May God bless you richly and favorably all your days – Coach "D."

THE LEADER OF LEADERS

THE CALL TO
SALVATION!

Those of you who desire to be leaders after the model of Jesus Christ will find that you must first take the lead in your own lives in submitting to the leadership of the Lord and Savior. You need to commit to a life of faith in Jesus Christ as your own Savior and Lord. You must believe that Jesus is Who and What he says that He is, God came to earth in the form of a man who lived a life totally without sin and who died on the cross as a sacrifice to satisfy God's justice for your sins. You must make that decisive commitment to God and accept His salvation through Jesus Christ. The way to do this is to express all this to God, to turn your life over to God and invite Jesus Christ to live in your heart and guide the direction of your life. If you say this to God, and mean it, He will come and live with you, and give you eternal life. Here is a prayer you may use:

Dear Lord God, I confess to you that I am in need of you as my Lord and my Savior. I am unable to lead myself, let alone anyone else, because my life is not in submission to the Leader of us all, Jesus Christ. I confess that I am a sinner in my heart and have committed many sins. I repent of these sins and ask that my sins be forgiven because Jesus paid the price for them in

His death on the cross. It was I, not He, who deserved that death. I now commit to follow Him, and trust that He will lead me in a righteous life, after which He will take me to live with Him forever.

In the Name of Jesus, who is God Himself,

(You may sign here.)

ISBN 141208913-1